Money Mastery In Your 20s

Ultimate Guide To Financial Freedom

Jenny Rick

TABLE OF CONTENTS

CHAPTER 1

Introduction

Why Start Early?

In your 20s, you have a unique and powerful advantage when it comes to building wealth and establishing financial independence. Early action sets the stage for long-term financial success, and the habits you develop now will shape your future. In this chapter, we'll explore why starting early matters and how you can leverage the benefits of youth, including the power of compound growth, the financial edge that comes with youth, and developing a success-oriented mindset that will guide your journey.

The Power of Compound Growth

One of the most compelling reasons to start your financial journey in your 20s is the power of compound growth. Compounding means that the money you invest not only grows by itself over time but that the returns on those investments are also reinvested, generating even more growth.

Starting early allows you to benefit from years of compounding, which can make a massive difference in your wealth over the long term.

For instance, investing just a small amount regularly in your 20s can grow substantially by the time you retire. Here's a simple example: if you invest $100 each month starting at age 20, with an annual return rate of 7%, that small contribution can grow to over $230,000 by age 60. But if you start investing that same amount at 30, you'd end up with only around $110,000 by age 60. The difference highlights how starting early can double, or even triple, your savings by retirement age.

Reflection Question

What would a financially free future look like for you, and how would compounding help you achieve it?

The Financial Advantage of Youth

Being young comes with several financial advantages. In your 20s, you typically have fewer financial responsibilities, which gives you more freedom to invest and take calculated risks.

This is the time to experiment, explore, and find the right path that will work for you without the weight of a mortgage, children's education, or retirement healthcare costs.

Youth also brings flexibility. You have the option to try different income-generating opportunities—side hustles, investments, or even entrepreneurship. With fewer constraints, you can afford to be more aggressive in building multiple streams of income that will serve you well in the future. And because time is on your side, you can recover from mistakes more easily, learn, and recalibrate without losing momentum.

Action Step

Identify two or three ways you could take advantage of the flexibility and time you have in your 20s to build wealth.

Shaping a Mindset for Success

Mindset is foundational to achieving financial success. Starting early gives you a prime opportunity to develop a growth-oriented, resilient mindset. To succeed financially, you'll need to cultivate self-discipline, delayed gratification, and a sense of purpose.

Rather than focusing solely on immediate rewards, learn to prioritize long-term goals that align with your vision for a successful life.

Embracing a mindset for financial success means understanding that this journey is more of a marathon than a sprint. There will be wins, setbacks, and adjustments along the way, but maintaining a resilient, adaptable attitude will keep you on track. Surround yourself with resources that encourage growth—books, mentors, and peers who share similar goals. As you shape this mindset, you'll find that good financial habits become easier to build and maintain, and your goals start feeling more achievable.

Quote

"The journey of a thousand miles begins with a single step."
– Lao Tzu

Practical Step

Write down your top three financial goals and why each goal is important to you. Keep these as a reminder of your purpose and vision.

Starting early gives you the head start most people wish they had. With the power of compound growth, the financial advantage of youth, and a success-driven mindset, you'll be setting yourself up for a prosperous and fulfilling future. Let's dive in and make these early years count!

CHAPTER 2

Financial Foundations

Understanding Money Mindset and Attitude

Your beliefs about money—shaped by family, culture, and past experiences—directly influence your financial decisions. Developing a healthy, growth-oriented money mindset is crucial for long-term success. This section will guide you in identifying limiting beliefs and adopting a perspective that fosters financial growth and resilience.

Expanding Your Money Mindset

Think about the people who have shaped your views on money. What messages did you receive about spending, saving, or investing?

If you think, "Money is hard to come by," challenge that thought by finding examples where you've succeeded financially or where you can improve your earning potential.

Create positive money mantras by replacing limiting beliefs with affirmations like "I am capable of achieving financial security."

Visualize success by spending a few minutes each day imagining what financial freedom looks like for you. Visualization can improve motivation and reinforce positive attitudes.

Defining Financial Success for Yourself

Financial success is personal—it means different things to different people. Rather than following someone else's definition, outline your own financial goals and aspirations based on what truly matters to you. This step is essential for creating a financial roadmap that resonates with your values and lifestyle.

Examples of Financial Goals

➢ Short-Term Goals: Building an emergency fund, paying off credit card debt.
➢ Long-Term Goals: Homeownership, early retirement, or travel funds.

Exercises for Clarity

- List Your Priorities

Identify and rank financial goals that matter most to you. Consider goals for the next year, five years, and beyond.

- Align Goals with Values.

Think about why each goal is important and how it supports your ideal life vision. This alignment strengthens your commitment to saving and investing with purpose.

Assessing Your Current Financial Situation

A clear understanding of your financial status is the cornerstone of effective money management. By assessing your income, expenses, debt, and savings, you'll gain insights that allow you to set achievable goals and pinpoint areas for improvement.

Getting a Clear Financial Picture

Income

Include all sources, including part-time work, investments, and side hustles.

Expenses

Separate needs from wants, and identify any subscriptions or habits that drain money.

Debt

List balances, interest rates, and monthly payments. Knowing your total debt load is crucial for creating a debt repayment plan.

Savings & Investments

Review your current balance, frequency of deposits, and any potential growth strategies.

Steps for Analysis

- Calculate Your Net Worth

Add up your assets (savings, property) and subtract liabilities (debts). This gives a snapshot of your financial health.

- Track Monthly Spending

For at least one month, keep a detailed record of every purchase.

At the end of the month, categorize your expenses to see where your money goes. Are there areas where you can cut back?

Creating a Basic Budget

Budgeting doesn't have to be restrictive. It's a tool to help you direct money toward what matters most to you. Start with a simple budget format that includes your main expenses, savings goals, and any discretionary spending.

Budgeting Strategies

50/30/20 Rule: Allocate 50% of your income to needs, 30% to wants, and 20% to savings or debt repayment.

Zero-Based Budgeting: Plan for every dollar you earn, giving each a purpose. This approach can help reduce unnecessary spending.

Action Plan

Set Monthly Savings Targets: Determine a savings target based on your income and goals. Automate this process if possible to ensure consistency.

Adjust Spending Habits

Based on your tracked spending, adjust your budget to prioritize savings and debt repayment.

Quote to Reflect On

"Money, like emotions, is something you must control to keep your life on the right track." — Natasha Munson

Reflection Questions

- How has your mindset about money helped or hindered your financial success so far?
- What is one financial habit you can start today that would improve your current situation?

Recommended Reading

- The Psychology of Money by Morgan Housel
- Rich Dad Poor Dad by Robert Kiyosaki

Action Steps Recap

- Write down any limiting beliefs and replace them with positive money affirmations.

- Assess your financial picture by listing assets, debts, income, and expenses.
- Start a simple budget, aiming to save or invest a percentage of your income each month.

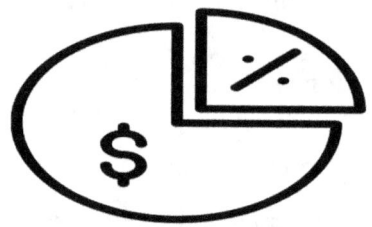

CHAPTER 3

Budgeting Basics

Budgeting might sound restrictive, but in reality, it's one of the most empowering steps you can take toward achieving financial independence. A practical budget is like a roadmap for your money, giving you a clear direction and showing you where to adjust your course when necessary.

To build a budget that truly works, it's important to start by fully understanding your current financial picture and defining your goals. This chapter will guide you through each stage of building a budget, tracking expenses, and finding the budgeting method that best aligns with your life.

Building a Practical Budget You Can Stick To

A successful budget begins with a clear grasp of your monthly income and all your expenses. Your income isn't just what's left after taxes; consider any side gigs, investments, or other income sources you might have. Expenses fall into two main categories: fixed expenses like rent, utilities, insurance, and loan payments, and variable expenses such as groceries, transportation, and entertainment.

Listing out these items not only shows you where your money is currently going but also clarifies areas where you might have flexibility for adjustments. The concept of needs versus wants is essential here. Needs are the essentials for basic living, like housing, food, and healthcare, while wants include non-essentials like eating out or upgrading your phone.

While it's tempting to spend on wants, a balanced budget often means curbing discretionary spending to free up funds for savings or investments. After laying out your income and expenses, identify realistic financial goals that keep you motivated. If you want to save for a trip, start an emergency fund, or build up a retirement account, knowing exactly how your budgeting efforts contribute toward those goals will make sticking to your budget feel more rewarding. A successful budget should also allow room for flexibility.

Life is unpredictable, and sometimes unexpected expenses come up, so setting aside a small "buffer fund" can help you stay on track even when surprises arise.

Tracking Expenses and Identifying Spending Habits

Once you have your budget outlined, tracking expenses is the next step to ensure you're staying on course. Think of expense tracking as a tool for holding yourself accountable. Many people start with manual tracking using a notebook or a spreadsheet, while others find budgeting apps that sync with their bank accounts helpful. Choose the method that feels easiest to maintain, as consistency is key. When you track expenses down to the last dollar, you can get an honest view of where your money really goes, which is often eye-opening.

Review your spending periodically to identify patterns and potential problem areas. For instance, you may notice that small, regular expenses, like a daily coffee or frequent rideshares, can add up quickly. Spotting these patterns allows you to see where small adjustments can lead to big savings.

If you find that you're consistently overspending on dining out, for example, setting a monthly limit on restaurants or trying meal-prepping can help curb costs without making you feel deprived.

Ultimately, the goal of tracking expenses is not to make you feel guilty, but to give you control, letting you prioritize what matters most to you while minimizing spending on things that don't bring as much value to your life.

The 50/30/20 Rule and Other Budgeting Methods

Once you understand your spending habits, choosing a budgeting framework can help guide your financial decisions. One of the most popular methods is the 50/30/20 rule: 50% of your income goes towards needs, 30% towards wants, and 20% for savings and investments. This approach is simple yet effective because it doesn't require extensive tracking of every purchase, which can be easier to maintain over the long term. For instance, if you earn $3,000 monthly, allocate $1,500 for essentials like rent and groceries, $900 for discretionary spending like hobbies or dining out, and $600 for saving or investing.

However, the 50/30/20 rule isn't the only budgeting method available, and some may find other approaches a better fit. If you prefer more structure, consider zero-based budgeting, where every dollar is assigned a purpose, so your income minus expenses equals zero.

This method requires a close look at all income and expenses, ensuring each dollar is accounted for. Alternatively, the envelope system can be useful if you like a more tangible method: cash is divided into labeled envelopes for each category, and once the money in an envelope runs out, you stop spending in that category for the month. This system is particularly helpful for controlling variable spending like entertainment or dining out.

Another flexible approach is pay-yourself-first budgeting, which prioritizes savings before expenses. This method involves setting aside a portion of your income for savings and investments as soon as you're paid, leaving the remainder for expenses. Paying yourself first ensures that you're putting money towards your goals before other spending occurs. Try different approaches, and don't be afraid to blend methods if that works best for you.

Sticking to Your Budget and Adjusting as Needed

Once you've set up your budget, the challenge is sticking to it. Treat it as a living document rather than something set in stone. Monthly check-ins and quarterly reviews are great for assessing whether you're on track.

If you realize that you've consistently overspent in one area or under-budgeted in another, it's okay to make adjustments. Real-life events, like unexpected car repairs or medical expenses, may mean adjusting your goals temporarily. Remember, the purpose of budgeting is to work with your life, not against it.

Another useful strategy is to use reminders to stay accountable. Setting calendar notifications to review your budget or keeping a daily spending log can help reinforce new habits. Over time, as you achieve small financial wins, you'll build confidence and momentum, making it easier to stick with the process.

Building a Practical Budget You Can Stick To

1. Define Your Income and Expenses

- **Income**

Calculate all sources of income, including salary, side jobs, or allowances. This is your baseline for creating a workable budget.

- **Expenses**

List out every expense, both fixed (like rent and insurance) and variable (like groceries and entertainment). Being honest about what you're spending will help you build a realistic budget.

2. Separate Needs vs. Wants

Breaking down needs and wants clarifies essential expenses versus discretionary spending. Essential expenses are things like rent, utilities, and groceries, while wants might include dining out, subscriptions, and shopping. Distinguishing between the two is essential to making your budget sustainable.

3. Automate Where Possible

Automating payments for fixed expenses like rent or loan repayments helps you stay consistent and avoid late fees. Set up automatic transfers into savings accounts as well to simplify your financial management.

Budgeting might not always be easy, but with a solid understanding of your income, mindful tracking of expenses, and a budgeting method that suits your lifestyle, you can gain control over your finances and take a major step towards financial freedom.

Quote to Reflect On

"A budget is telling your money where to go instead of wondering where it went." — Dave Ramsey

Reflection Questions

- Which budgeting method aligns best with your lifestyle and spending habits?
- Are there any expenses you're willing to reduce or cut to reach your financial goals faster?

Resources and Further Reading

- The Total Money Makeover by Dave Ramsey
- You Need a Budget by Jesse Mecham

Action Steps Recap

- Choose a budgeting method that resonates with you.

- Track your spending for the next month, and review areas where adjustments could be made.

- Set up automatic payments or transfers to make budgeting easier and more consistent.

CHAPTER 4

Saving The Right Way

In your 20s, the financial choices you make carry a tremendous weight, setting the tone for the financial habits and security you'll build over a lifetime. One of the core foundations of financial stability is saving. While often overlooked, saving early is the stepping stone to achieving your financial goals, allowing you to prepare for both opportunities and unexpected expenses with confidence.

Why Saving Early Matters

The importance of saving early can't be overstated. Saving in your 20s, even in small amounts, has a compounding effect that can substantially increase your wealth over time. Compounding is the principle where the interest you earn generates more interest, growing your initial investment exponentially. Starting early allows even modest savings to grow into significant sums over time, leveraging the years ahead to build wealth.

Beyond financial growth, saving early nurtures a mindset of financial responsibility and discipline.

It teaches you to prioritize your goals, delay unnecessary gratification, and secure yourself against uncertainties. By making saving a priority now, you're not only investing in your future but also empowering yourself to seize opportunities as they arise without financial strain.

Setting Up Emergency Funds

An emergency fund is your financial safety net, and creating one should be a top priority. Life is unpredictable, and unexpected expenses—whether they're medical bills, car repairs, or sudden job changes—can disrupt your financial stability if you're unprepared. An emergency fund ensures you're covered without having to rely on debt or compromise your long-term savings.

➢ Determine Your Emergency Fund Goal

A typical guideline is to save enough to cover three to six months' worth of living expenses. Start by calculating your monthly essentials—housing, utilities, groceries, transportation, and healthcare. Multiply this amount by your target months of coverage (e.g., 3-6 months). If you're just starting out, aim for at least one month's worth of expenses and build from there.

➢ Open a Separate, Accessible Savings Account

To avoid dipping into your emergency fund for non-emergencies, it's wise to keep it separate from your regular checking account. A high-yield savings account or money market account can be a good choice, as these accounts offer better interest rates and easy access when needed.

➢ Start Small, but Be Consistent

Building an emergency fund can seem daunting, especially if you're managing multiple financial goals. Start by contributing a small amount each month, even if it's just $50. Regular contributions add up, and as you increase your income or manage your budget better, you can gradually raise the amount.

➢ Replenish After Use

If you do need to tap into your emergency fund, make it a priority to rebuild it as soon as possible. Consistently replenishing it ensures you're always prepared, no matter what life throws your way.

Automating Savings and Building Consistency

Automating your savings is one of the most effective ways to maintain a consistent saving habit. By setting up automatic transfers from your checking account to your savings account, you can save without even thinking about it. Automation removes the mental burden of deciding to save each month, ensuring that saving is prioritized no matter what expenses come your way.

➤ Set a Savings Goal

Decide on a specific amount to save each month based on your income, budget, and financial goals. Even small, consistent contributions can grow significantly over time.

➤ Schedule Automatic Transfers

Many banks and financial apps allow you to set recurring transfers. For example, if you get paid on the first and fifteenth of each month, schedule an automatic transfer to your savings account on those dates. This "pay yourself first" approach ensures your savings are deducted before other expenses.

➢ Monitor and Adjust

As your financial situation evolves, review and adjust your savings amount. If you get a raise, allocate a portion of it to savings. Conversely, if you're facing financial challenges, you can temporarily reduce your savings amount without breaking the habit entirely.

➢ Consider Round-Up Features

Many banking apps offer a round-up feature that rounds each purchase to the nearest dollar and saves the difference. Though small, these amounts can add up over time, providing an effortless way to increase your savings.

By automating your savings, you're establishing a habit that reinforces financial discipline and creates a foundation for long-term success.

Practical Steps to Saving

Open a Separate Savings Account: This allows you to differentiate your funds and reduces the temptation to spend your savings.

- Calculate Your Savings Goal

Define your emergency fund goal and monthly savings target.

- Set Up Automatic Transfers

Schedule automatic deposits into your savings account for consistency.

- Use Round-Up Apps

Activate round-up features to save small amounts from everyday purchases.

- Track and Celebrate Milestones

Mark each milestone—such as reaching $500, $1,000, or one month's worth of expenses—to stay motivated.

Quote to Reflect On

"Do not save what is left after spending, but spend what is left after saving." — Warren Buffett

This quote reinforces the importance of prioritizing savings and setting aside funds before addressing other expenses. By placing savings first, you ensure that financial security is built into your budget rather than treated as an afterthought.

Reflection Questions

- What motivates me to save? Identify the goals and dreams that make saving meaningful to you.
- How much can I realistically save each month? Assess your current budget and determine a feasible savings target.
- What would I do if I faced a financial emergency today? Consider whether you feel financially secure and how an emergency fund could provide peace of mind.

Resources and Further Reading

Books

- The Simple Path to Wealth by JL Collins
- Your Money or Your Life by Vicki Robin and Joe Dominguez

Financial Websites:

- NerdWallet for savings account comparisons and budgeting tools
- Mint.com for personal finance management and expense tracking.

Apps:

- Qapital: A savings app with automated transfers and round-up features.
- YNAB (You Need a Budget): A robust app for budgeting and saving.

Action Steps Recap

- Start an Emergency Fund: Open a separate account dedicated to emergencies and set a target goal.
- Automate Your Savings: Schedule recurring transfers from your checking account to your savings.
- Practice Consistent Saving: Even if you start small, commit to saving regularly and gradually increase your contributions.

- Track Your Progress: Monitor your savings balance and celebrate small milestones along the way.

- Stay Motivated: Reflect on your reasons for saving, and revisit your goals periodically to keep your efforts aligned with your aspirations.

In establishing a strong savings habit, you're building the foundation of your financial independence. While saving in your 20s may seem challenging, the rewards—security, freedom, and peace of mind—are well worth the effort. Each dollar saved brings you one step closer to financial resilience and the ability to pursue your dreams on your terms.

CHAPTER 5

Debt Management and Avoidance

In your 20s, understanding debt and how to manage it is crucial. Debt can either be a tool for growth or a burden that limits your financial freedom. Many young adults enter their working years with student loans or other debts, making it easy to feel overwhelmed or constrained by these financial commitments. However, by learning to manage debt wisely and adopting strategies to avoid excessive borrowing, you can maintain financial flexibility and build a foundation for future wealth.

Understanding Good Debt vs. Bad Debt

Not all debt is inherently negative. While high-interest debt, such as credit card balances, can quickly drain your resources and limit your financial options, other forms of debt—such as student loans or a reasonable mortgage—can be considered "good debt." Good debt is often low-interest and has the potential to increase your net worth by funding education, property, or business opportunities.

By discerning between good and bad debt, you can make more informed financial decisions that support your long-term goals.

➢ Good Debt

Typically low-interest debt that supports investments, like student loans, mortgages, or small business loans. These debts can help increase your income potential or build your assets.

➢ Bad Debt

Often high-interest and associated with non-essential purchases, such as credit card debt or personal loans for consumer items. Bad debt does not contribute to your financial growth and can lead to financial strain if not managed carefully.

Strategies for Managing Debt Wisely

1. Know Your Debt Details: Start by listing all your current debts, including credit card balances, student loans, car loans, or personal loans. Record each debt's balance, interest rate, minimum payment, and due date.

Understanding your debt landscape will allow you to prioritize and make a realistic plan for repayment.

2. Prioritize High-Interest Debt: Focus on paying off high-interest debts first, as these accumulate quickly and make it harder to break free from financial strain. By allocating extra payments toward high-interest debts, you reduce the total amount paid in interest over time, accelerating your journey to becoming debt-free.

3. Use the Snowball or Avalanche Method:

➢ Snowball Method: Focus on paying off the smallest debt first, then apply that payment amount to the next debt, creating momentum and a sense of accomplishment.

➢ Avalanche Method: Prioritize debts with the highest interest rates first. This approach saves you more in the long run by reducing interest payments but may take longer to see progress.

4. Avoid Minimum Payments When Possible: Paying only the minimum may keep your account in good standing, but it leads to paying more interest over time.

Whenever possible, aim to make more than the minimum payment to reduce both your balance and interest payments.

5. Refinance or Consolidate When Advantageous: If you have multiple high-interest debts, consolidating them into a lower-interest loan or refinancing high-interest loans can save you money. Research and compare options to see if consolidation will provide a lower monthly payment or better interest rate.

Strategies for Avoiding Debt

1. Build a Budget and Stick to It: A solid budget helps you live within your means, reducing the need to rely on credit. Allocate funds for essentials, savings, and entertainment, so that you can comfortably cover your expenses without resorting to borrowing.

2. Create an Emergency Fund: An emergency fund reduces the need to rely on debt when unexpected expenses arise. Start by saving for small emergencies, like car repairs or medical expenses, and gradually work toward three to six months' worth of expenses.

3. Limit Credit Card Usage: Credit cards can be convenient but also tempting. To avoid falling into debt, use your credit card only for planned expenses that you can pay off in full each month. Avoid carrying a balance, as credit card interest is typically high.

4. Adopt a Cash-First Mindset: Make it a rule to save up for purchases rather than buying on credit. A cash-first approach helps you avoid unnecessary debt and makes you more intentional about your spending.

5. Invest in Financial Literacy: Knowledge is power. By learning about interest rates, credit scores, and debt management, you make wiser financial decisions that support your goals. Many free resources and courses are available to help you improve your understanding of personal finance.

Practical Steps for Managing and Avoiding Debt

➢ Create a Debt Repayment Plan

List all your debts, prioritize them, and decide on a repayment method—Snowball or Avalanche—that fits your situation.

➢ Make Extra Payments Whenever Possible

Direct any extra income, such as bonuses or side gig earnings, toward your debt to reduce balances faster.

➢ Commit to Minimal Credit Card Usage

Only use your credit card for planned expenses and pay off the balance monthly.

➢ Save for Major Purchases

Delay large purchases until you've saved enough to buy them with cash, avoiding unnecessary debt.

➢ Reevaluate Spending Regularly

Track your budget and spending habits to ensure you're consistently living within your means.

Quote to Reflect On

"Debt is An ingenious substitute for the chain and whip of the slave driver." — Ambrose Bierce

This quote emphasizes the importance of avoiding unnecessary debt to maintain personal freedom and financial autonomy.

By managing debt responsibly, you free yourself from financial stress and maintain control over your financial choices.

Reflection Questions

- What types of debt do I currently have, and how do they impact my financial goals?
- How would being debt-free improve my life?
- What can I do differently to reduce my reliance on debt?

Resources and Further Reading

Books

- The Total Money Makeover - by Dave Ramsey
- I Will Teach You to Be Rich - by Ramit Sethi

Websites

- National Debt Relief: Provides tips and resources for debt repayment and management.
- NerdWallet: Offers calculators, articles, and comparisons of financial products for debt management.

Apps

- Debt Payoff Planner: An app that helps you track debt repayments using the Snowball or Avalanche methods.

- Mint: Personal finance app that can help with budgeting, tracking expenses, and managing debt.

Action Steps Recap

➢ Understand Your Debt

Make a list of your debts and categorize them by interest rate and priority.

➢ Choose a Repayment Strategy

Select either the Snowball or Avalanche method and commit to it.

➢ Limit Credit Card Use

Use credit only for planned expenses that you can pay off immediately.

> Build a Debt-Free Lifestyle

Shift to a cash-first mentality, creating an emergency fund and living within your means.

> Invest in Financial Knowledge

Learn more about debt management, interest rates, and budgeting to make informed decisions.

Taking control of your debt in your 20s empowers you to focus on building wealth and financial security rather than being weighed down by repayments. By mastering debt management strategies and adopting a mindful approach to borrowing, you can pave the way to a future of financial freedom and opportunities.

CHAPTER 6

Investing for Dummies

Investing in your 20s can have a profound impact on your financial future, giving you a head start in building wealth and achieving financial freedom. Unlike saving, which preserves money with little growth potential, investing actively grows your wealth, leveraging time and compound returns. Though it may seem intimidating initially, learning the basics of investing early can open up a lifetime of financial possibilities.

Why Start Investing Now?

Starting to invest in your 20s comes with one major advantage: time. Time is the most valuable asset in investing, as it allows compound interest to work its magic. Compound interest, the phenomenon of earning returns on your initial investment and the earnings it generates, creates exponential growth over time. The earlier you start, the less money you need to invest to reach your goals, thanks to compounding.

Time Is Money

The longer you leave your money invested, the more it grows, thanks to compounding. This means that someone who invests early can achieve the same growth with much less initial capital than someone who starts later.

Learning Curve

Investing young gives you the freedom to learn, make mistakes, and adjust your approach without the urgency many experience in later years when retirement looms closer.

Risk Tolerance

Younger investors generally have a higher risk tolerance since they have more time to recover from market downturns. This allows them to pursue potentially higher-yield investments like stocks, which can offer significant growth over the long term.

Investment Options for Beginners

- **Stocks**

Buying stocks means purchasing shares in a company, making you a part-owner. Stocks are riskier than other asset classes but offer higher potential returns. For beginners, starting with index funds or ETFs, which bundle various stocks, can be a great way to minimize risk while gaining exposure to the market.

- **Bonds**

Bonds are essentially loans you give to corporations or governments. They're considered safer than stocks but offer lower returns. Bonds are ideal for stabilizing an investment portfolio, especially during market fluctuations.

- **Mutual Funds and ETFs**

Mutual funds pool money from multiple investors to buy a diversified portfolio of stocks, bonds, or other securities. Exchange-Traded Funds (ETFs) operate similarly but are traded on the stock market, allowing you to buy and sell them like individual stocks. Both are great options for beginners seeking diversification.

- **Real Estate**

Investing in property can yield both income and long-term appreciation. While buying real estate may require more capital, Real Estate Investment Trusts (REITs) provide a way to invest in real estate without buying property directly.

- **Retirement Accounts (401(k) and IRA)**

These accounts offer tax benefits that help your investments grow faster. Employer-sponsored 401(k)s often come with matching contributions, while Individual Retirement Accounts (IRAs) provide flexibility for those without a 401(k) option.

Getting Started with Investing

Set Clear Financial Goals.

Before investing, know what you're aiming to achieve. Are you investing for retirement, a down payment on a house, or financial independence? Different goals may require different approaches, time horizons, and risk tolerance.

Next determine your risk tolerance.

Are you comfortable with the ups and downs of the stock market, or do you prefer more stable investments? Knowing your risk tolerance helps you choose the right mix of assets, balancing growth potential with your comfort level.

Establish an Emergency Fund First

Before you invest, ensure you have at least three to six months' worth of expenses saved. This cushion prevents you from having to sell investments in emergencies, which could lock in losses during market downturns.

Start Small and Consistent

Many beginner investors believe they need a large sum to get started. In reality, you can start investing with as little as $50 per month. Consistency is key; regular contributions add up over time, and dollar-cost averaging helps reduce the impact of market volatility.

Consider Robo-Advisors and Investment Apps

For beginners, robo-advisors and investment apps like Acorns, Betterment, or Vanguard offer low-cost, automated investing options that tailor portfolios based on your goals and risk tolerance.

➢ Building a Balanced Portfolio

Diversification: Spreading investments across various asset types (stocks, bonds, real estate, etc.) reduces risk and smooths returns. Diversification is key to weathering market ups and downs without losing substantial value.

Over time, market fluctuations will affect the proportions of your portfolio. Rebalancing means adjusting your portfolio back to its original target allocation, ensuring it remains aligned with your risk tolerance and financial goals.

Avoid the temptation to react to short-term market changes. Investing for the long term means you don't have to worry about the day-to-day fluctuations of the market.

Practical Steps for Starting to Invest

Open an Investment Account

Start with a retirement account like a Roth IRA if you're self-employed or an employer-sponsored 401(k) if available. For other investments, open a brokerage account.

Choose a Beginner-Friendly Platform

Platforms like Vanguard, Fidelity, or Charles Schwab offer user-friendly options with low fees. Alternatively, consider robo-advisors if you prefer an automated approach.

Commit to a Monthly Contribution

Start small if necessary, but make it a goal to contribute to your investment account every month. Setting up automatic transfers helps make investing a habit.

Educate Yourself Continuously

Financial literacy is critical. Dedicate time each month to learning more about investing, whether through books, podcasts, or online courses.

Quote to Reflect On

"The best time to plant a tree was 20 years ago. The second best time is now." — Chinese Proverb

This quote reflects the importance of starting early with investing. Even if you didn't begin as early as possible, today is the next best opportunity to start building a foundation for financial independence.

Reflection Questions

- What financial goals are most important to me, and how can investing help me achieve them?
- What am I most hesitant about when it comes to investing, and how can I work through those fears?
- How can I make investing a consistent part of my financial routine?

Resources and Further Reading

Books:

- The Intelligent Investor by Benjamin Graham
- A Random Walk Down Wall Street by Burton G. Malkiel

Websites:

Investopedia: Offers articles and tutorials for investors at every level.

Morningstar: Provides investment research, including mutual fund and ETF reviews.

Apps:

Acorns: Invests your spare change automatically, making it easy to get started.

Stash: Helps beginners learn about investing and build a diversified portfolio.

Action Steps Recap

- Set Clear Goals: Define your financial goals and the purpose behind your investments.
- Determine Risk Tolerance: Understand your comfort level with investment risks and build a diversified portfolio accordingly.
- Open and Fund Your Account: Begin with an account that aligns with your goals, such as a Roth IRA or brokerage account.

- Educate and Rebalance: Dedicate time each month to learning more about investing, and periodically rebalance your portfolio.

Investing is one of the most powerful ways to build long-term wealth, and starting in your 20s can give you a unique advantage. By learning the basics, setting realistic goals, and maintaining a consistent investment habit, you set yourself on a path toward financial freedom and the opportunity to enjoy the benefits of wealth early in life.

CHAPTER 7

Building Wealth with Assets

Building wealth goes beyond saving money; it involves acquiring assets that grow in value and generate income over time. Assets like real estate, businesses, stocks, and other investments play a crucial role in creating a foundation for long-term wealth. This chapter explores the types of assets that can help you grow your net worth, build passive income streams, and secure your financial future.

What Are Assets, and Why Are They Important?

In financial terms, an asset is anything you own that has economic value and the potential to provide future benefits. Assets differ from liabilities, which are things that cost you money without offering a return. Building wealth through assets allows you to generate income and increase your net worth passively, giving you more financial freedom over time.

➢ Financial Security

Assets provide a cushion against financial instability. Unlike regular income, which stops if you're unable to work, assets can continue to grow and produce income.

➢ Passive Income Potential

Many assets, such as rental properties or dividend-yielding stocks, can generate passive income, meaning you earn money with minimal ongoing effort.

➢ Compound Growth

Investing in assets that appreciate in value allows you to benefit from compound growth. This means that your wealth can grow exponentially over time, especially if you reinvest your returns.

Types of Wealth-Building Assets

Real Estate

Real estate is one of the most popular assets for wealth building. It appreciates over time and can generate rental income.

Real estate can also be leveraged, allowing you to buy property with a mortgage, meaning a relatively small investment upfront can grow significantly in value.

Stocks and Bonds

Stocks represent partial ownership in a company, and bonds are essentially loans you give to corporations or governments. Stocks offer growth potential, while bonds provide more stability and regular income. Together, they form the backbone of many investment portfolios.

Business Ownership

Owning a business is a powerful way to build wealth. Whether you start a business or invest in someone else's, business ownership can generate significant returns. Successful businesses provide cash flow, appreciation in value, and can even offer tax advantages.

Intellectual Property (IP)

Intellectual property like patents, copyrights, or trademarks can generate income through royalties and licensing.

If you create something valuable, such as a book, a product design, or a song, it can provide residual income long after the initial work is done.

Precious Metals and Commodities

While not as growth-oriented as other assets, gold, silver, and other commodities can provide a hedge against inflation and economic instability. They add diversity to a portfolio, offering security in uncertain times.

Cryptocurrency

Digital assets like cryptocurrency offer high potential returns but come with high volatility. While crypto may not be the primary asset class for most beginners, some people include it in their portfolio for diversification and growth potential.

Getting Started with Building Wealth Through Assets

Decide what you want to achieve. Are you looking for income generation, appreciation, or both? Each asset class serves a different purpose in wealth building.

Now, determine how much you can invest. Some assets, like real estate, require a significant upfront investment, while others, like stocks or intellectual property, may have lower barriers to entry.

Diversify Your Portfolio

Avoid putting all your money into one asset class. Diversification allows you to spread risk across various assets, increasing the chances of stable returns.

Educate Yourself

Before investing, learn about each asset's risks, rewards, and requirements. Read books, take courses, and talk to people who have successfully invested in different asset classes.

Seek Professional Advice

Consulting with a financial advisor can help you make informed decisions, especially if you're considering complex assets like real estate or business investments.

Strategies for Building a Portfolio of Wealth-Building Assets

Start Small and Grow Consistently. Begin with assets that fit your budget and gradually increase your investments as your wealth grows. For example, start by investing in stocks before moving to larger assets like real estate.

Use Leverage Wisely

Leveraging means using borrowed capital to invest in assets, like purchasing real estate with a mortgage. While leverage can amplify returns, it also increases risk, so use it cautiously.

Reinvest Your Earnings

Compounding works best when you reinvest earnings from your assets. For instance, reinvest dividends from stocks or rental income from real estate to buy more assets.

Focus on Assets Aligned with Your Skills and Interests. If you enjoy working on homes, real estate might be a good fit. If you're passionate about technology, perhaps investing in tech stocks or startups will be fulfilling.

Be Patient and Persistent

Building wealth with assets takes time and consistency. Avoid the urge to jump in and out of investments based on short-term market fluctuations. Stick to your long-term plan.

Practical Steps to Begin Building Wealth with Assets

Research and Select Your First Asset

If you're new to investing, start with stocks or mutual funds through a reliable brokerage. For those looking at real estate, consider researching low-cost options like real estate investment trusts (REITs).

Allocate a Portion of Your Monthly Income for Asset Building

Decide how much you can set aside each month to invest in assets. Automating contributions to your investment accounts helps make asset building a habit.

Seek Out Investment Education Resources

Use online platforms, books, and courses to deepen your understanding. Some popular resources include Investopedia, The Motley Fool, and various financial literacy podcasts.

Monitor and Rebalance Your Portfolio

Review your asset performance periodically and make adjustments as needed to stay aligned with your goals.

Quote to Reflect On

"Do not save what is left after spending, but spend what is left after saving." — Warren Buffett

This quote captures the essence of prioritizing wealth-building activities. By focusing on investing in assets before spending, you set yourself up for financial security and freedom.

Reflection Questions

- What types of assets interest me most, and why?
- How much risk am I comfortable taking with each type of asset?
- What steps can I take now to start building wealth through assets?

Resources and Further Reading

Books

- Rich Dad Poor Dad by Robert Kiyosaki
- The Millionaire Real Estate Investor by Gary Keller

Websites

- BiggerPockets: A platform for real estate investment education.
- NerdWallet: Offers information on a variety of asset types and investment strategies.

Apps

- Robinhood: Easy access to stocks and ETFs with no fees.
- Fundrise: Allows you to invest in real estate with low minimums.

Action Steps Recap

- Define Your Goals: Decide on the financial outcome you want from your assets, whether it's income generation or long-term growth.

- Choose Your First Asset Class: Select an asset type that matches your risk tolerance, starting capital, and interest.

- Automate Investments: Set up automatic contributions to your investment accounts to build wealth consistently.

- Monitor Progress: Regularly review your portfolio and make adjustments as needed to stay aligned with your financial goals.

Building wealth through assets is a foundational step toward financial freedom. By understanding the different types of assets, establishing clear financial goals, and investing consistently, you can create a wealth-building system that works for you now and grows with you into the future.

CHAPTER 8

Building Passive Income Streams

Passive income is one of the most effective ways to achieve financial freedom, allowing you to earn money without active effort on a continuous basis. While it often requires an upfront investment—either of time, money, or both—once established, passive income can provide consistent returns and increase financial security. This chapter delves into how you can create and maintain various passive income streams, ranging from investments to entrepreneurial ventures.

Understanding Passive Income and Its Benefits

Passive income is income earned from ventures in which you are not actively involved on a day-to-day basis. Unlike active income, which requires direct effort to earn (like a job or a freelance gig), passive income generates revenue in the background, providing financial stability and additional opportunities for wealth building.

➢ Financial Independence

Passive income allows you to depend less on a primary job for financial security, giving you the freedom to pursue interests without financial constraints.

➢ Increased Wealth Over Time

With passive income, you can reinvest earnings into additional income streams or investments, enabling compound growth and creating a strong foundation for future wealth.

➢ Time Flexibility

Earning passive income means you are not bound by traditional work schedules, granting you more time to focus on personal goals, travel, family, or even build new passive income streams.

Introduction to Passive Income Ideas

1. Dividend-Yielding Investments: Investing in dividend stocks or mutual funds allows you to earn a portion of company profits, which are distributed regularly as dividends. These earnings can be reinvested to purchase additional shares, growing your portfolio over time.

2. Real Estate Rentals: Owning rental properties is a popular way to generate passive income. Rental properties provide monthly income from tenants and appreciate over time, offering a stable and growing revenue stream.

3. Royalties from Intellectual Property: If you're creative or knowledgeable in a specific field, consider creating intellectual property, such as books, music, or online courses. Royalties from these assets can provide residual income long after the initial work is done.

4. Peer-to-Peer Lending: Platforms like Lending Club and Prosper allow you to lend money to individuals or small businesses in exchange for interest payments. Though riskier than traditional investments, peer-to-peer lending can yield higher returns if managed wisely.

5. Automated E-commerce: Starting an e-commerce store through platforms like Shopify or Amazon FBA, or creating a print-on-demand business, allows you to sell products with minimal management. Once established, you can automate operations for a steady income.

6. Real Estate Investment Trusts (REITs): REITs are companies that own, operate, or finance income-generating real estate. By investing in REITs, you can earn a share of income produced without the responsibility of managing properties.

7. Affiliate Marketing: Affiliate marketing involves promoting other companies' products online and earning a commission on sales. Once set up, affiliate links can continue to generate revenue as people make purchases through your recommendations.

Passive Income Ideas

- **Freelancing**

Freelancing on Platforms like Fiverr and Upwork is a gateway to building passive income. By taking on projects in areas such as graphic design, writing, or consulting, you can establish an online reputation. Over time, creating pre-packaged services, such as downloadable resources or templates, can generate passive income.

- **Online Businesses and E-Commerce**

Starting an online store using platforms like Shopify or Amazon FBA allows you to sell products to a global audience. Dropshipping, for example, minimizes the need for inventory, making it easier to manage while focusing on marketing and growth. Automate processes like customer service and order tracking for a more hands-off income stream.

- **Self-Publishing on Amazon KDP**

Publishing your own book or eBook on platforms like Amazon Kindle Direct Publishing (KDP) opens up an income stream with minimal ongoing effort. After the initial creation and publishing, books continue to sell as long as they meet reader demand. Many authors build a reliable income by releasing multiple books on topics within their expertise.

- **Content Creation (YouTube, Podcasting, Blogging)**

Creating a YouTube channel, podcast, or blog allows you to reach audiences interested in your knowledge or hobbies.

Once monetized through ads, sponsorships, or affiliate links, these platforms can generate income long after the content is uploaded. With consistent quality content, your subscriber or listener base can grow, leading to a steady revenue stream.

- **Course Creation**

If you're skilled in a particular area, creating and selling online courses on platforms like Udemy or Teachable can be a profitable way to share your expertise. Once created, courses require minimal upkeep but continue generating revenue as new students enroll. Updating courses occasionally keeps them relevant and attractive to future learners.

Getting Started with Passive Income Streams

➢ Identify Your Interests and Strengths:

Think about areas where you have knowledge or experience. For example, if you understand investing, dividend stocks or REITs may be suitable. If you enjoy content creation, a blog or YouTube channel for affiliate marketing might be ideal.

➢ Assess Initial Costs and Time Investment

Each passive income stream has unique startup requirements. Some, like stock investments, primarily require capital. Others, like e-commerce or content creation, demand upfront time to create and establish.

➢ Research and Educate Yourself

Each passive income avenue has specific risks, rewards, and strategies. Reading books, taking online courses, and connecting with successful individuals in the field can provide valuable insights.

➢ Start Small and Scale Gradually

Begin with one stream that aligns with your budget and skillset. As your income grows, diversify into other streams for added stability and growth potential.

➢ Focus on Quality and Consistency

Whether it's a rental property or an affiliate website, providing quality—such as reliable tenant service or useful product recommendations—ensures that your income stream remains stable and potentially grows over time.

Practical Steps for Building Passive Income

1. Choose Your First Passive Income Stream

Begin with one stream that suits your skillset and financial situation. For instance, start investing in dividend stocks with a small amount or consider developing an eBook if you're skilled in writing.

2. Invest Consistently

Passive income often requires regular investment, whether that's money, time, or resources. Create a schedule for contributing to your chosen income stream, whether it's saving for a rental property down payment or adding new affiliate links to a blog.

3. Automate When Possible

Automation is essential for maximizing passive income. For example, use online platforms that automatically reinvest dividends or set up marketing automation tools for e-commerce stores.

4. Track and Adjust

Monitor your passive income streams to see what's performing well and what could use improvement. Make adjustments as necessary, such as reinvesting earnings or exploring more profitable options.

Quote to Reflect On

"If you don't find a way to make money while you sleep, you will work until you die." — Warren Buffett

Buffett's advice underscores the importance of creating passive income. By establishing sources of income that operate independently of your time, you build financial security that sustains itself.

Reflection Questions

1. Which passive income stream interests me the most, and why?

2. What resources (time, money, skills) do I have to invest in building passive income?

3. How can I balance the risks and rewards associated with each income stream I'm considering?

Resources and Further Reading

Books

  - Passive Income, Aggressive Retirement by Rachel Richards

  - The 4-Hour Workweek by Tim Ferriss

Action Steps Recap

- Identify Your Interest Area: Select a passive income stream that aligns with your interests and skills.

- Start Small: Begin with manageable contributions or initial investments to get started.

- Automate Earnings: Look for ways to automate the income generation process, freeing up more time.

- Reinvest and Grow: Use earnings from one stream to fund additional passive income opportunities, diversifying and increasing your earnings potential.

Passive income streams are instrumental for building financial freedom and wealth. By choosing the right mix of income sources, you can create a reliable and growing foundation of revenue, enabling you to live life on your terms and work toward lasting financial independence.

CHAPTER 9

Financial Discipline and Goal Setting

In the journey to financial freedom, discipline and clear goals are essential. Without them, even the best financial strategies can falter. Financial discipline involves building consistent habits that align with your objectives, while goal setting helps you define what you want to achieve. In this chapter, we'll discuss how to set SMART financial goals, build habits for long-term success, and stay motivated in pursuit of your financial dreams.

Setting SMART Financial Goals

SMART goals—Specific, Measurable, Achievable, Relevant, and Time-bound—are particularly effective for personal finance. Setting SMART goals provides structure and clarity, helping you stay focused on actionable, realistic targets. Here's a breakdown:

➢ **Specific**

Vague goals like "save more" are hard to measure or achieve. A specific goal would be "Save $5,000 for a down payment on a car.

➢ **Measurable**

Quantify your goal so you can track your progress. For instance, "Save $200 per month" gives you a clear measure to hit.

➢ **Achievable**

While aiming high can be motivating, unrealistic goals often lead to frustration. If you're new to budgeting, set manageable milestones rather than trying to save 50% of your income immediately.

➢ **Relevant**

Align your financial goals with your personal values and future aspirations. If travel is a priority, set a savings goal to fund your adventures.

> **Time-bound**

Attach deadlines to your goals. Instead of saying, "I want to save for retirement," specify, "I want to have $20,000 saved in my retirement account by age 30.

When setting financial goals, consider both short-term and long-term objectives. Short-term goals, like saving for a laptop or building an emergency fund, help you develop discipline and build confidence. Long-term goals, such as retirement or home ownership, keep you focused on the bigger picture.

Building Consistent Habits for Long-Term Success

Achieving financial goals isn't a single action but a collection of habits. Creating a system of small, sustainable habits is essential for long-term success. Here's how to start building a habit system that supports your financial goals:

- Start Small

Implement small actions that don't overwhelm you, like saving $20 each week. Small steps build consistency, making it easier to stay on track over time.

- Automate Financial Tasks

Automating your savings, investments, and bill payments reduces the need for constant decision-making. For example, set up an automatic transfer to your savings account each payday. This keeps your financial goals on track without needing constant reminders.

- Review and Adjust

Regularly reviewing your financial habits allows you to make adjustments as needed. If you're finding it difficult to save a specific amount each month, adjust to a more achievable level rather than stopping altogether. Consistency is key, even if progress is slower than expected.

- Celebrate Milestones

Recognizing progress along the way can reinforce good habits. When you reach a financial milestone, reward yourself with a small treat or simply take time to acknowledge your efforts.

Staying Motivated and Focused on Financial Objectives

Long-term financial success requires sustained motivation. Over time, it's easy to lose sight of your goals, especially when immediate gratification is tempting. Here are some strategies for maintaining motivation:

1. Visualize Success

Picture the future benefits of your financial goals. Imagine the freedom of a debt-free life, the excitement of travel, or the security of a well-funded retirement. Visualization reinforces why you're working hard and sacrifices are worthwhile.

2. Use a Support System

Surround yourself with friends, family, or mentors who support your financial goals. Accountability partners can help you stay disciplined and motivated, while sharing ideas and successes can keep you inspired.

3. Track Progress with a Journal or App

Tracking your achievements can boost motivation. Use a financial app or journal to record your progress, noting down small wins as you work toward larger goals. Seeing progress over time can make setbacks feel manageable and motivate you to stay the course.

4. Accept Setbacks as Part of the Journey

Financial goals don't always go perfectly to plan. Unexpected expenses or missed targets are common, but they don't have to derail your progress. Instead of feeling discouraged, treat setbacks as learning experiences and adjust your approach if needed.

Practical Steps to Building Financial Discipline

1. Define Your Goals: Write down clear, specific, and time-bound financial goals. Start with a mix of short- and long-term objectives that align with your values.

2. Automate Your Savings: Set up automated transfers into savings or investment accounts. This reduces the temptation to spend money intended for savings.

3. Track Your Spending and Adjust Habits: Review your expenses monthly to identify spending patterns. Adjust your budget to align spending with your financial goals.

4. Celebrate Small Milestones

Reward yourself when you hit a savings target or achieve a financial goal. Celebrations, even small ones, reinforce good habits.

Quote to Reflect On

"Discipline is the bridge between goals and accomplishment." – Jim Rohn

Reflection Questions

1. What are my most important financial goals, and why are they meaningful to me?

2. Which small habit can I implement today to bring me closer to my goals?

3. How will I stay motivated when challenges arise, and what support can I rely on?

Resources and Further Reading

Books

- Atomic Habits by James Clear

Apps

- Mint: For budgeting and expense tracking.

- YNAB (You Need a Budget): To help establish and stick to a budgeting system.

Websites

- Dave Ramsey: Practical insights on budgeting and debt management.

- Financial Independence Subreddit: A community with tips and motivation for staying on track.

Action Steps Recap

- Define SMART Financial Goals: Be specific, measurable, achievable, relevant, and time-bound.

- **Automate to Build Discipline**: Set up automatic transfers to savings and investment accounts.

- Track, Adjust, and Stay Consistent: Review your spending and make adjustments as needed.

- Stay Motivated with Visualization and Support: Use visualization, accountability partners, and milestone celebrations to stay on track.

With strong financial discipline and clear goals, you create a foundation for lasting financial success and freedom. This discipline not only leads to wealth but also brings you closer to the life you envision for yourself.

CHAPTER 10

Financial Mistakes to Avoid

As young adults navigate their 20s, they often find themselves at a crossroads, filled with opportunities yet fraught with potential pitfalls. This is a decade marked by newfound independence, but it can also be a time of significant financial mistakes. Recognizing these common pitfalls is essential to ensuring a healthier financial future.

Many young people fall into the trap of living beyond their means. As income increases, whether from a new job or a side hustle, there's a temptation to upgrade lifestyles—luxury dinners, trendy clothes, and the latest tech gadgets. It's easy to lose sight of the importance of budgeting when every paycheck feels like a ticket to spend freely. However, distinguishing between wants and needs is vital. The thrill of a new purchase can quickly fade, while the burden of financial stress lingers far longer.

Ignoring debt is another common misstep. As student loans pile up and credit card balances grow, the instinct is often to bury one's head in the sand.

The feeling of being overwhelmed can lead to avoidance, but this only exacerbates the situation. The interest on loans can spiral out of control if not managed promptly. A proactive approach to debt management—one that includes creating a repayment plan and sticking to it—can turn this daunting challenge into a manageable task.

In this age of instant gratification, neglecting savings is a mistake that many young adults make. The power of compound interest is a tool that can work wonders, but only if savings begin early. Imagine the peace of mind that comes from having an emergency fund—money set aside to cover unexpected expenses like car repairs or medical bills. Establishing this cushion can prevent the need to rely on credit cards during crises, helping to avoid the debt trap.

Budgeting often feels tedious, yet it's one of the most powerful tools for financial health. Without a clear understanding of income and expenses, it's easy to overspend. Many young adults overlook the benefits of budgeting tools and apps designed to simplify this process.

These resources can provide insights into spending habits, enabling informed decisions about where to cut back and how to allocate funds wisely.

Education plays a crucial role in avoiding financial mistakes. Unfortunately, many young adults embark on their financial journeys without sufficient knowledge about personal finance. Relying on trial and error can lead to costly lessons. Investing time in understanding financial principles—such as how to manage credit, the importance of diversification, and the benefits of retirement accounts—can prevent serious missteps down the line. Learning from the mistakes of others can be just as valuable as recognizing one's own missteps.

Scenerios

"Take the case of Alex, a bright college graduate who found himself drowning in credit card debt shortly after graduation. Initially, he felt invincible, swiping his card for dinners, outings, and the latest tech. It wasn't long before he realized that the thrill of those purchases came with a price. His monthly statements revealed the reality of his financial situation—a staggering balance that felt insurmountable.

Alex's journey became a cautionary tale, teaching him the importance of budgeting and mindful spending. His experience is a reminder that every financial decision counts and can have long-lasting effects."

"Maria's story also serves as a powerful lesson. Enthusiastic about building wealth, she invested her savings in a flashy "get-rich-quick" scheme without conducting thorough research. The excitement of potential high returns clouded her judgment. As she watched her hard-earned money disappear, Maria learned a painful lesson about the importance of due diligence. This experience highlighted the need for careful consideration before making financial commitments, reinforcing the idea that not all opportunities are worth pursuing."

"Jake's experience offers another perspective on financial growth. He frequently jumped from job to job, chasing higher pay without considering the long-term implications of his choices. While his salary increased, he missed out on valuable benefits like retirement plans and career development opportunities.

Eventually, he realized that a stable career path could provide more significant financial security in the long run. This insight emphasizes the value of planning for the future and weighing the benefits of immediate gratification against long-term rewards."

When faced with financial setbacks, it's crucial to know how to pivot and recover. If you find yourself in a challenging situation—whether due to unexpected expenses, a job loss, or a failed investment—take a step back to assess the circumstances. What led to the setback? Did you overspend during a moment of weakness, or did an unforeseen expense catch you off guard? Understanding the root cause is essential for creating a plan to move forward.

Creating a recovery plan can be a transformative process. It might involve tightening your budget, cutting unnecessary expenses, or exploring new income opportunities. Consider side jobs or freelance work to supplement your income during tough times. Each small step taken toward recovery can build momentum, gradually restoring your financial footing.

Sometimes, seeking professional help can make all the difference. A financial advisor can provide personalized guidance, helping you develop a sustainable financial plan tailored to your goals. They can offer strategies for debt repayment, investment opportunities, and effective budgeting techniques. Partnering with an expert can empower you to make informed decisions and regain control of your financial journey.

Above all, embracing a growth mindset is essential. Instead of viewing financial setbacks as failures, learn to see them as valuable lessons. Each misstep offers an opportunity to reassess your financial goals and strategies. Use setbacks as stepping stones to greater financial resilience and adaptability.

To avoid common financial mistakes, consider implementing practical steps in your daily life. Start by creating a monthly budget that clearly outlines your income and expenses. This tool can help you track your spending and identify areas for improvement. Establishing an emergency fund should also be a priority.

Aim to save at least three to six months' worth of living expenses, providing a safety net for unforeseen circumstances.

Setting clear financial goals can maintain your focus and motivation. Define both short-term and long-term objectives, whether it's saving for a vacation, paying off debt, or planning for retirement. Regularly review these goals to stay accountable and make adjustments as necessary.

Education is a lifelong journey, especially when it comes to personal finance. Seek out resources that can enhance your understanding of financial principles. Books, online courses, and workshops can provide valuable insights and strategies for managing your money effectively.

Reflecting on your financial journey is crucial. Take the time to consider the mistakes you've made and what you've learned from them. What financial missteps have shaped your perspective? How can you apply the lessons learned to your current situation? Embrace these reflections as opportunities for growth and improvement.

To reinforce your learning, consider these reflection questions:

- What financial mistakes have I made in the past, and what did I learn from them?
- How can I apply lessons from others' financial mistakes to my own life?
- What steps can I take today to pivot from a current financial setback?

As you navigate your financial journey, keep the following resources in mind:

- The Total Money Makeover by Dave Ramsey offers practical strategies for debt elimination and budgeting.
- Your Money or Your Life by Vicki Robin provides insights into transforming your relationship with money.
- Rich Dad Poor Dad by Robert Kiyosaki explores the importance of financial education and investing.
-

By being mindful of common financial mistakes, learning from the experiences of others, and developing strategies for recovery, you can set yourself up for a brighter financial future. Remember that every decision you make today shapes your tomorrow. Embrace the journey with an open mind, and let your experiences guide you toward lasting financial well-being.

Practical Steps to Avoid Financial Mistakes

Create a Monthly Budget: Use tools like spreadsheets or budgeting apps to track income and expenses effectively.

Establish an Emergency Fund: Aim to save at least 3-6 months' worth of living expenses to cover unexpected costs.

Set Financial Goals: Define short-term and long-term goals to maintain focus and motivation.

Educate Yourself: Read books, take online courses, and attend workshops to improve your financial literacy.

Review Your Credit Report: Regularly check your credit report to understand your credit health and identify areas for improvement.

Quote to Reflect On

"It's not how much money you make, but how much money you keep, how hard it works for you, and how many generations you keep it for." — Robert Kiyosaki

Action Steps Recap

1. Review your current financial situation and identify areas for improvement.

2. Create or update your budget.

3. Establish a plan for managing and reducing debt.

4. Set realistic financial goals for the next month and year.

5. Continue to educate yourself on personal finance through books and resources.

CHAPTER 11

Preparing for the Future

As your 20s come to a close and the realities of adulthood set in, the importance of preparing for the future becomes increasingly clear. This chapter serves as a guide to anticipating major life events, ensuring a secure financial future, and addressing health and insurance needs. Taking proactive steps now can set the foundation for a life filled with opportunity and stability.

Planning for Major Life Events

Life in your 20s is often a whirlwind of experiences—graduating from college, starting a career, and possibly considering significant milestones like buying a home or starting a family. These life events can be exciting but also come with financial implications that require careful planning.

Buying a home is one of the most significant purchases many will make in their lifetime. It symbolizes stability and achievement, yet the journey to homeownership can be fraught with challenges. The first step is to understand the costs involved, which go far beyond the purchase price. You'll need to factor in property taxes, insurance, maintenance, and potential homeowners' association fees. Begin by saving for a down payment, which can often range from 5% to 20% of the home's price. It's essential to create a budget that prioritizes these savings alongside your regular expenses.

Consider the importance of improving your credit score as well. A higher credit score can lead to better mortgage rates, ultimately saving you thousands over the life of the loan. Monitor your credit regularly, paying down existing debts, and making sure to pay bills on time. In addition to financial readiness, it's crucial to research neighborhoods and understand the housing market in your desired area. Knowledge is power, and being informed will help you make wise decisions.

Starting a family is another significant life event that requires financial preparation. The joys of parenthood are accompanied by a range of expenses, from prenatal care to childcare, education, and healthcare.

Begin by assessing your current financial situation and establishing a budget that accommodates these new costs. Look into health insurance options that cover maternity care and pediatric visits, as well as potential savings accounts for education, like 529 plans.

Conversations with your partner about family planning can also help align your financial goals and expectations. Discussing savings for future needs and planning for emergencies can foster a sense of teamwork and collaboration in this new chapter of life.

Setting Up Retirement Accounts Early

While it may seem premature to think about retirement in your 20s, this is precisely the time to start laying the groundwork for a secure financial future. The earlier you begin saving for retirement, the more time your money has to grow through compound interest. Even small contributions can accumulate significantly over the years.

Consider setting up a retirement account, such as a 401(k) or an Individual Retirement Account (IRA). If your employer offers a 401(k) plan, take full advantage of any matching contributions—this is essentially free money that can exponentially increase your retirement savings. Aim to contribute at least enough to meet the employer match, then gradually increase your contributions as you can.

If you choose an IRA, explore the differences between a Traditional IRA and a Roth IRA. A Traditional IRA allows for tax-deductible contributions, while a Roth IRA offers tax-free withdrawals in retirement. Understanding these options and selecting the right account based on your financial situation can have a significant impact on your long-term savings.

Make retirement savings a priority, even if it means making sacrifices in other areas. This might involve cutting back on discretionary spending, such as dining out or impulse purchases, in favor of building a retirement nest egg. Automate your savings by setting up direct deposits into your retirement accounts; this strategy ensures you're consistently contributing without the temptation to spend those funds.

Preparing for Health and Insurance Needs

As you move through life, preparing for health and insurance needs becomes paramount. Life is unpredictable, and having a comprehensive plan in place can alleviate stress during challenging times.

Begin by assessing your current health insurance coverage. Understand what your policy includes and whether it meets your needs, especially as you consider starting a family. Research various plans and providers to find options that offer adequate coverage for your lifestyle, including maternity care, routine check-ups, and specialist visits. Open enrollment periods are your opportunity to make changes, so stay informed about deadlines and options available to you.

Health savings accounts (HSAs) can also be beneficial, particularly if you have a high-deductible health plan. An HSA allows you to set aside pre-tax money for medical expenses, and these funds can grow tax-free over time. The flexibility of an HSA makes it a valuable tool for managing healthcare costs now and in the future.

In addition to health insurance, consider other types of insurance, such as life insurance and disability insurance. Life insurance can provide peace of mind for those with dependents, ensuring they are financially supported in the event of an unexpected tragedy.

Disability insurance offers protection against the loss of income due to injury or illness. Evaluating your individual circumstances can help you determine which types of insurance are right for you.

Practical Steps to Preparing for the Future

As you prepare for major life events, consider these practical steps to secure your financial future:

➢ Establish a Home-Buying Budget

Create a detailed budget that outlines all costs associated with homeownership, including down payment, mortgage, and ongoing expenses. Start saving early to reach your down payment goal.

➢ Research Neighborhoods

Investigate potential neighborhoods to find the right fit for your lifestyle and budget. Attend open houses and engage with local real estate agents to gain insight into the housing market.

➢ Create a Family Budget

If you plan to start a family, develop a comprehensive budget that considers all costs associated with raising children. Factor in healthcare, childcare, and education expenses.

➢ Set Up Retirement Accounts

Open a 401(k) or IRA as early as possible, aiming to contribute regularly. Take advantage of employer matches and consider increasing your contributions over time.

➢ Evaluate Insurance Needs

Assess your health insurance coverage and explore options for life and disability insurance. Ensure you have adequate coverage to protect yourself and your loved ones.

Quote to Reflect On

"The future depends on what you do today." — Mahatma Gandhi

Reflection Questions

- What major life events do I anticipate in the next few years, and how can I financially prepare for them?

- How can I incorporate retirement savings into my current budget?
- What steps can I take today to ensure I have adequate health and insurance coverage in the future?

Resources and Further Reading

- The Bogleheads' Guide to Investing by Taylor Larimore, Mel Lindauer, and Laura F. Dogu
- The Simple Path to Wealth by JL Collins

Websites

National Association of Realtors (for home buying resources), HealthCare.gov (for health insurance options)

Action Steps Recap

- Start saving for a home by establishing a budget and creating a dedicated savings account.
- Research neighborhoods and understand the housing market.
- Create a family budget that includes potential childcare and education expenses.

- Set up retirement accounts and automate contributions.

- Evaluate and adjust your health and insurance needs regularly.

CHAPTER 12

Financial Literacy and Continuous Learning

Financial literacy is a lifelong journey. Just as industries and economies evolve, so does the world of personal finance. Staying informed, continuing to learn, and expanding your financial knowledge is essential to navigate life's twists and turns successfully. This chapter explores ways to deepen your financial understanding, connect with like-minded individuals, and remain informed in a dynamic economic landscape.

Books, Courses, and Resources for Financial Education

When it comes to financial knowledge, there's a wealth of resources available to suit every learning style—whether you're a reader, a visual learner, or someone who benefits from interactive experiences. Financial literacy begins with a strong foundation, and books are an accessible, flexible way to start building it.

Classic titles like *Rich Dad Poor Dad* by *Robert Kiyosaki* introduce readers to concepts like assets versus liabilities, while *The Total Money Makeover* by *Dave Ramsey* covers budgeting and debt management from a practical standpoint. For a broader perspective, *The Intelligent Investor* by *Benjamin Graham* offers insights into the principles of value investing.

If you're interested in more structured learning, online courses offer interactive and practical ways to expand your knowledge. Platforms like **Coursera, Udemy, and Khan Academy** provide financial courses that range from budgeting basics to advanced investment strategies. Many of these courses are taught by industry experts, including financial planners, investment analysts, and professors, ensuring that you receive high-quality instruction. Some even offer certificates, which can add credibility to your knowledge if you're looking to apply it in a professional setting.

In addition to books and courses, podcasts are a powerful tool for continuous learning. Programs like *The Dave Ramsey Show*, *Afford Anything by Paula Pant*, and

ChooseFI offer real-life insights into managing money, investing, and building wealth. These shows feature discussions with financial experts, success stories from people who have reached financial independence, and practical tips you can apply to your own life. Podcasts are also convenient for multitasking, allowing you to learn on the go.

Beyond individual resources, consider subscribing to financial publications like *Forbes, The Wall Street Journal, or Financial Times*. These outlets provide up-to-date information on market trends, economic events, and personal finance tips, keeping you informed about changes that could impact your financial strategy.

Building a Network of Financially Savvy Peers

Surrounding yourself with financially knowledgeable peers is a powerful way to accelerate your growth. Imagine having friends or colleagues who can offer insights on investments, share budgeting tips, or introduce you to new financial resources.

A network of financially savvy individuals not only offers advice and support but can also provide accountability, helping you stay focused on your financial goals. You can start building this network by joining financial education groups, whether online or in-person. Websites like Reddit and Facebook have communities dedicated to personal finance topics where you can engage in discussions, ask questions, and share your knowledge.

For more structured networking, consider attending finance-related meetups, seminars, or workshops in your area. Many cities host regular events where you can connect with other financially minded individuals, exchange ideas, and learn about new financial strategies.

If you're interested in a more intensive experience, look into joining a mastermind group. These are small, goal-oriented groups that meet regularly to discuss progress, offer guidance, and share resources. Mastermind groups are particularly effective for those committed to serious financial goals, as the consistent support and accountability can help you overcome challenges and maintain momentum.

Mentorship is another valuable aspect of networking. Finding a financial mentor—someone who has successfully managed their finances and achieved a degree of financial stability—can provide you with personalized guidance. Many mentors offer insights that aren't found in books or courses, sharing lessons learned from real-life experiences. Look within your network, or reach out to professionals on platforms like LinkedIn, who may be open to offering mentorship.

The Importance of Staying Informed

In a world where economic conditions shift frequently, staying informed is crucial. Changes in interest rates, inflation, tax laws, and investment options can all impact your financial plans. Being proactive about understanding these shifts helps you make informed decisions, adjust your strategies, and seize new opportunities as they arise.

Staying informed begins with daily habits. Make it a routine to check the financial news each morning, even if it's just for a few minutes. Look at headline news that covers economic updates, such as interest rate changes from the Federal Reserve, or new tax policies that could affect your income and investments.

Understanding these elements helps you adjust your strategy if needed, whether that means rebalancing your investment portfolio, adjusting your retirement contributions, or revisiting your budget.

Financial blogs are also a great resource. Websites like *NerdWallet, Investopedia, and Money Under 30* offer articles that break down complex financial topics into easy-to-understand language. Following these blogs keeps you informed about new financial products, emerging trends, and best practices for managing your money.

Consider subscribing to financial newsletters as well, which often include tips, analysis, and summaries of the most relevant financial news. Many well-known finance professionals, like Ramit Sethi and Morgan Housel, offer newsletters that provide valuable insights and practical advice. These can be particularly useful if you're interested in topics like behavioral finance, which examines how emotions and biases can affect financial decisions.

Finally, take the time to review your financial goals and strategies regularly. Financial literacy isn't just about learning new concepts; it's about applying that knowledge in a way that aligns with your goals. Schedule a quarterly "financial check-up" to assess your progress, evaluate any changes in your personal circumstances, and update your strategies as needed.

Practical Steps for Financial Literacy and Continuous Learning

To maintain a high level of financial literacy, consider these practical steps:

➢ Create a Financial Reading List

Choose a few books each year to deepen your financial understanding. Aim for a balance between classics and current bestsellers to cover both foundational principles and contemporary insights.

➢ Enroll in Online Courses

Take a financial course each quarter to expand your knowledge. Topics can range from budgeting to investment strategies, giving you a well-rounded understanding of personal finance.

> ➤ Subscribe to Financial News Sources

Keep up with financial publications and websites to stay informed about economic changes that could impact your finances.

> ➤ Join Financial Groups and Forums

Engage with online communities where you can discuss personal finance topics, ask questions, and exchange ideas.

> ➤ Attend Financial Workshops and Seminars

Look for local or virtual events to connect with financially savvy individuals and build a supportive network.

Quote to Reflect On

"An investment in knowledge pays the best interest." — Benjamin Franklin

Reflection Questions

1. What are my preferred learning methods, and how can I use them to expand my financial knowledge?

2. Who are the financially savvy individuals in my life that I can learn from or network with?

3. How can I make staying informed about finance and economics a part of my daily routine?

Resources and Further Reading

- The Millionaire Next Door by Thomas J. Stanley and William D. Danko

- Financial Freedom by Grant Sabatier

- Websites: NerdWallet, Investopedia, and Money Under 30

- Podcasts: ChooseFI and Afford Anything

Action Steps Recap

1. Start building a reading list of finance-related books and resources.

2. Enroll in an online finance course to develop a deeper understanding of key topics.

3. Join online financial communities and consider attending local finance-related events.

4. Create a habit of reviewing financial news and updates regularly.

CHAPTER 13

The Road to Financial Freedom

Achieving financial freedom is a journey that requires continuous growth, consistent reassessment, and a clear vision of what you want your life to look like. As you progress, you'll find that your financial goals and strategies evolve, reflecting changes in your life, career, and values. This chapter focuses on refining your financial strategy, knowing when to adjust your goals, and cultivating a mindset that supports lifelong financial growth.

Reviewing and Refining Your Financial Strategy

As you move forward on the path to financial freedom, it's essential to periodically review and refine your financial strategy. Just like any journey, the path to financial independence can encounter unexpected turns, and the original strategies that worked for you might no longer be as effective. Regularly reassessing your financial plan allows you to stay aligned with your evolving goals and current circumstances.

Start by analyzing your income and expenses. Are you making more than when you first started your journey? Has your spending changed? Perhaps you've paid off some debts, or maybe new expenses, such as a mortgage or family costs, have emerged. With each stage of life, a financial check-up can help you understand if your budget and goals are still realistic. Reviewing your spending categories, savings rate, and investment performance ensures you stay on track to achieve your larger objectives.

As part of this review, examine your investment portfolio as well. Diversification and risk tolerance are fundamental aspects of a solid investment strategy, yet they may need adjusting as your wealth grows or as market conditions fluctuate. For example, as you approach significant life events like purchasing a home or planning for retirement, you might choose to transition to lower-risk investments.

Alternatively, if you're young and have a longer time horizon, you might decide to pursue growth-focused assets. Keep in mind that staying informed about market trends and economic shifts can aid in making educated adjustments to your portfolio.

One powerful tool in refining your financial strategy is the habit of automating your finances. By setting up automatic transfers into savings and retirement accounts, you remove the temptation to overspend and guarantee that your money is working toward your goals. Regular automatic contributions to investment accounts allow you to take advantage of dollar-cost averaging, reducing the impact of market volatility over time.

Knowing When to Adjust Your Goals

On the journey to financial freedom, it's natural for goals to evolve. Life is full of unexpected opportunities and challenges, and the financial objectives you set in your 20s or 30s may no longer reflect your values, priorities, or needs as you grow older. Recognizing when to adjust your goals is crucial to maintaining motivation and making progress toward financial independence.

Re-evaluating your goals begins with an honest assessment of your current situation and future aspirations. Ask yourself questions like: Have I reached a major milestone, such as paying off debt or achieving a certain level of savings?

Am I facing new priorities, such as buying a home, starting a family, or transitioning to a new career? Taking the time to reflect on these shifts ensures that your financial plan remains relevant and supportive of your life's direction.

For example, early on, your primary goal might have been to build an emergency fund or pay off student loans. Once you've reached these milestones, you may decide to prioritize goals like investing more aggressively, saving for a down payment, or even working towards early retirement. Some individuals find that as their financial situation improves, they want to redirect funds towards causes or activities they're passionate about, such as philanthropy or pursuing personal interests.

This shift might mean adjusting how much you allocate to different savings or investment goals, ensuring that your plan aligns with your current and future priorities.

Financial freedom isn't about rigidly sticking to a plan; it's about creating a strategy that supports your evolving life. Knowing when to pivot—whether it's due to a career change, family growth, or even a new perspective on what "freedom" means to you—allows you to stay committed to goals that genuinely matter.

Embracing a Mindset of Financial Growth

Achieving financial freedom isn't only about reaching a certain net worth or eliminating debt. It's about cultivating a mindset that fosters continuous learning, flexibility, and a sense of abundance. Embracing a growth-oriented mindset means viewing money as a tool for expanding possibilities rather than a source of stress or restriction.

A mindset of financial growth begins with understanding that wealth-building is a gradual process. By focusing on steady, incremental progress rather than instant results, you create sustainable habits that support your financial journey. Celebrate small victories along the way, such as reaching savings milestones or making wise investment choices. Recognizing these achievements can help you stay motivated and resilient, especially during challenging times.

Another key to a growth-oriented mindset is openness to learning. Stay curious and proactive about expanding your financial knowledge, whether that means exploring advanced investing techniques, understanding tax strategies, or learning about emerging opportunities like sustainable investing. Regularly reading books, attending seminars, or listening to finance podcasts can provide fresh insights that inspire and inform your strategies.

Additionally, adopting a long-term perspective is crucial to maintaining a positive financial outlook. Market downturns, unexpected expenses, or changes in income can be discouraging, but a resilient mindset allows you to weather these challenges without losing sight of your goals. Over time, you'll come to see these moments as learning experiences that ultimately strengthen your financial approach.

Financial freedom is also about cultivating a sense of balance and gratitude. While wealth-building requires discipline, it's equally important to enjoy the fruits of your labor. Treating yourself periodically, celebrating with loved ones, or investing in experiences that bring joy can keep you grounded and remind you of the true purpose of financial independence.

Practical Steps on the Road to Financial Freedom

In this journey toward financial freedom, consider these practical steps to help keep you on course:

➢ Schedule Regular Financial Reviews

Set aside time each quarter or year to review your budget, savings rate, and investments. This ensures your financial strategy remains aligned with your life goals.

➢ Refine Your Goals

Evaluate your current financial objectives. Adjust your savings, investments, or budget to reflect any new priorities or life changes.

➢ Automate and Simplify

Automate as much of your financial life as possible to ensure consistent progress. Use automatic transfers and bill payments to streamline your finances.

➤ Prioritize Continuous Learning

Commit to expanding your financial knowledge by reading books, listening to finance podcasts, or taking courses. Staying informed can help you make educated decisions.

➤ Celebrate Your Wins

Recognize and celebrate milestones along the way. Achieving financial freedom is a journey, and celebrating small victories helps maintain motivation.

Quote to Reflect On

"The goal isn't more money. The goal is living life on your terms." — Chris Brogan

Reflection Questions

1. How often do I review my financial plan, and how well does it reflect my current goals?

2. In what ways can I simplify my financial life to stay focused on long-term growth?

3. How can I foster a mindset of continuous learning and resilience in my financial journey?

Resources and Further Reading

- Your Money or Your Life by Vicki Robin and Joe Dominguez

- I Will Teach You to Be Rich by Ramit Sethi

- Websites

Mr. Money Mustache, Financial Independence forums on Reddit

- Podcasts:

Financial Independence Podcast by the Mad Fientist,

Action Steps Recap

1. Conduct a regular financial review to assess your progress and realign your goals.

2. Update your financial goals to reflect current priorities and future aspirations.

3. Embrace automation to simplify saving, investing, and budgeting.

4. Prioritize learning opportunities to stay informed and adaptable in your financial journey.

CHAPTER 14

Early Money Mastery for Lifelong Success

The journey to financial independence is more than just achieving specific monetary milestones. It's about crafting a life where money serves as a tool for freedom, flexibility, and fulfillment. By taking charge of your financial future early, you're building habits and mindsets that will serve you for a lifetime. As you stand at the finish line of this book, you have gained insights, strategies, and motivation to master your finances. This is a moment to celebrate how far you've come, to look forward with purpose, and to inspire those around you to join the path toward financial empowerment.

Celebrating Progress and Future Possibilities

Every milestone reached along your financial journey is worth celebrating. Whether it's paying off a debt, reaching a savings goal, or making your first investment, each accomplishment brings you one step closer to the freedom and security you desire.

Reflecting on these successes is essential, not just to acknowledge the hard work but also to reinforce the habits and choices that made them possible. By recognizing each step, you reinforce the idea that financial freedom is not a single event but an accumulation of small, wise decisions over time.

Celebration doesn't have to be extravagant; it can be as simple as sharing your accomplishments with loved ones, treating yourself to something meaningful, or simply taking a moment to reflect on how much you've grown. Allow yourself to feel proud of the sacrifices and dedication it took to achieve these goals. Looking back at the progress you've made, no matter how small, reminds you of the potential for even greater achievements in the future. This sense of fulfillment will keep you motivated, guiding you through new challenges and motivating you to reach even higher.

Now that you've established a strong financial foundation, the future possibilities are limitless. Imagine what financial independence can mean for you: the ability to travel, to retire early, to pursue passions, or to simply live without the burden of financial stress.

By mastering your finances, you open doors to opportunities that align with your values and dreams. You're no longer just working for money; your money is working for you.

Staying Committed to Financial Independence

While celebrating progress is vital, the path to lifelong financial success is a continuous commitment. Financial independence doesn't mean reaching a single endpoint where all financial concerns disappear; it's an ongoing journey that requires diligence and adaptability. Economic conditions change, life throws unexpected curveballs, and your personal priorities may evolve over time. Staying committed means remaining proactive, informed, and willing to adjust your strategies as needed.

A cornerstone of this commitment is maintaining financial discipline. The habits you've built—saving consistently, budgeting carefully, and investing wisely—will continue to serve you well as long as you uphold them. Staying disciplined, however, doesn't mean depriving yourself. Instead, it's about making intentional choices that align with your goals.

The same mindfulness and intention that helped you get started will be essential to maintaining the stability and security you've worked so hard to create.

As you move forward, remember that the principles of financial independence are not static. Regularly review your financial goals and strategies. Assess your investments, reconsider your budget, and stay informed about new financial tools and trends that could support your journey. Committing to lifelong learning in the realm of finance helps you stay adaptable, allowing you to adjust your plans to meet new challenges and seize new opportunities.

Encouraging the Next Generation in Financial Literacy

One of the greatest gifts you can share is the knowledge you've gained about financial literacy. While you've worked hard to build your own financial independence, inspiring others to do the same helps create a cycle of empowerment and education. Sharing what you've learned with the next generation—whether that's younger family members, friends, or even your own children—can have a profound impact on their lives.

Start by introducing basic financial concepts to younger individuals in a way that's relatable and accessible. Talk to them about budgeting, saving, and the value of planning for the future. Sharing your own experiences, both successes and mistakes, can make financial literacy more relatable and give others the confidence to start their own journey. Encouraging the next generation to take an interest in their finances helps build a culture of financial empowerment and responsibility, extending the benefits of your hard work far beyond your own life.

Consider leading by example. Model the financial habits you wish to pass on, and show others the importance of setting and working towards goals. Mentorship, whether formal or informal, can be a powerful way to help others develop a solid financial foundation. Direct others to resources—books, websites, and courses—that have been helpful in your journey, making it easier for them to start learning.

By encouraging financial literacy in the next generation, you're contributing to a future where more individuals have the knowledge, skills, and confidence to take charge of their financial lives.

This legacy of empowerment ensures that the values of financial freedom and independence live on, creating a ripple effect that can positively impact countless lives.

Practical Steps for Lifelong Financial Success

To help you sustain your progress and inspire others, here are a few practical steps:

➢ Celebrate Your Milestones

Regularly acknowledge the progress you've made, whether it's reaching savings goals, paying off debts, or making successful investments. This helps reinforce positive financial habits.

➢ Commit to Ongoing Learning

Continue expanding your financial knowledge by staying updated on new tools, trends, and strategies. Make financial literacy a lifelong practice.

➢ Encourage Financial Literacy in Others

Share your experiences and knowledge with those around you, especially younger individuals, to foster a culture of financial empowerment.

> ➤ Adapt as Life Changes

Regularly review and adjust your financial goals to stay aligned with your evolving life circumstances and aspirations.

Quote to Reflect On

"Financial freedom is available to those who learn about it and work for it." — Robert Kiyosaki

Reflection Questions

1. How will I continue to celebrate my financial achievements without losing sight of my long-term goals?

2. What steps can I take to stay committed to financial independence and adaptability?

3. How can I best encourage financial literacy and empowerment in those around me?

Resources and Further Reading

- Rich Dad Poor Dad by Robert Kiyosaki

- The Millionaire Next Door by Thomas J. Stanley and William D. Danko

- Financial literacy programs, such as Dave Ramsey's

- Financial Peace University or online resources like Khan Academy's finance courses

- Websites like Investopedia and Financial Independence blogs

Action Steps Recap

1. Celebrate your financial progress and acknowledge the habits that contributed to your success.

2. Remain committed to financial independence by adapting your goals and maintaining your habits.

3. Inspire the next generation by sharing your knowledge and encouraging financial literacy.

www.ingramcontent.com/pod-product-compliance
Lightning Source LLC
Chambersburg PA
CBHW071513220526
45472CB00003B/1011